RAF Manston
A Second Selection

IN OLD PHOTOGRAPHS

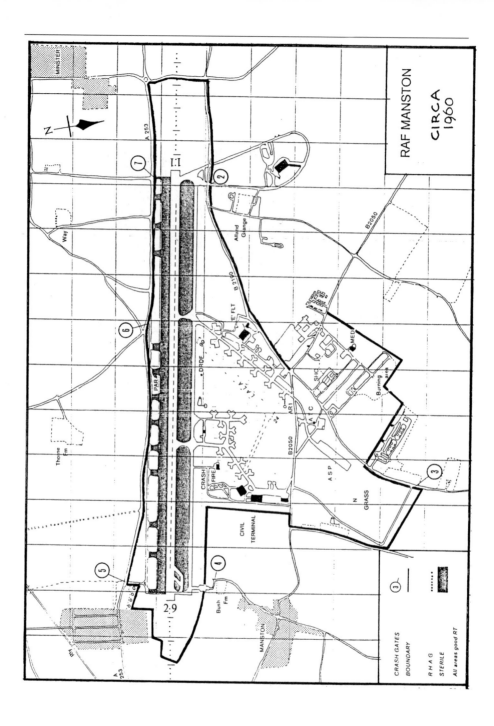

RAF MANSTON
CIRCA 1960

N

MINSTER

A 253

Way

Thorne Fm

Bush Fm

MANSTON

A 253

Altand Grange

B 2190

DRDE 90'

PAR

E FLT

L A A A A

24

ATC

AR1

SHQ

MED

Burning arch

B2050

B2050

ASP

N GRASS

CIVIL TERMINAL

CRASH FIRE

2.9

1:1

CRASH GATES

BOUNDARY

R H A G

STERILE

All areas good RT

2

RAF Manston
A Second Selection

IN OLD PHOTOGRAPHS

Collected by
RAF MANSTON HISTORY CLUB

Alan Sutton Publishing Limited
Phoenix Mill · Far Thrupp
Stroud · Gloucestershire

First published 1994

British Library Cataloguing in Publication Data.
A catalogue record for this book is available
from the British Library.

ISBN 7509–0705–3

Typeset in 9/10 Sabon.
Typesetting and origination by
Alan Sutton Publishing Limited.
Printed in Great Britain by
Redwood Books, Trowbridge.

Contents

Foreword

The present infrastructure of RAF Manston is itself a record of its history, with a range of buildings that originate from its very earliest days to some that were constructed during the late eighties. This book portrays a mixture of events at RAF Manston, both significant and routine, which have occurred in and around these buildings. Individually some of the events may appear of little consequence. However, together they help bring to life memories of the station, especially for those who have been associated with it over the years.

Manston is one of the few RAF stations, if not the only one, to have seen continuous service since 1916. Furthermore, its location has been geographically significant, not only during the two world wars but also, because of its proximity to the Continent, during the Cold War when, among other roles, it provided an arrival/departure point for many aircraft in transit between the forces stationed in Germany and the United Kingdom. The station has also hosted a search and rescue helicopter unit, under various guises, since July 1961. After thirty-three years, following a review of the UK search and rescue organization, the most recent unit, 'C' Flight No. 202 Squadron, finally departs to Wattisham in July 1994. It is therefore a particular pleasure for me that some of its activities at Manston are recorded within these pages.

Events at Manston, and specifically during the Battle of Britain, have been well documented elsewhere. However, the station has an active History Club, which includes Service and ex-Service personnel from the local community who share an interest in these events and the units and people involved, and which has built up an extensive library of photographs that add additional flesh to the records. The club's involvement with the station goes back to before the Second World War and thus, with the benefit of personal recollection, it is able to produce this proud and lively record of day-to-day events at Manston over the years.

The study of history is not just an academic pastime recording events in chronological order. It is primarily about people and how their activities contributed to and made history. It also provides an insight into the lives of those who experienced the events. I consider that this book achieves this particularly well, and my gratitude goes to the Service and ex-Service personnel and those friends of Manston who have helped put it together. It is most fitting that those closely associated with the station should be the recorders of its history; after all it is they and their successors who have and will continue to make it.

Wing Commander David White

Introduction

The history of aviation in the Manston area is linked not only with the activities of the British air services, as illustrated in our successful first volume, *RAF Manston in Old Photographs*, but with early flying and pioneering activities as a whole at such venues as Eastchurch and Shellbeach on nearby Isle of Sheppey. The area's close proximity to the Continent has also contributed to it being the scene of interesting aviation events well before Manston became an airfield in 1916. To that end, attention has been given in this second volume of photographs to several organizations not noted in the first volume, or barely so, who none the less played their part at or in association with Manston. The compilers have taken a look back to pre-First World War days and included photographs of people and events which excited much interest locally as well as looking in more detail at RAF Manston. We are confident readers will appreciate this further selection of relevant photographs.

Although the 1920s saw the 'Geddes Axe' bring severe cutbacks to the services and swingeing restrictions were widespread, Manston continued to operate busily with a variety of units and aircraft in residence or merely visiting. The period was also marked by important and sometimes dramatic aviation events which touched the base. For example, when the giant airship, R.101, crashed in France en route to India on 5 October 1930, the bodies of those so tragically killed were given a guard of honour, provided by RAF Manston, on their return to Dover. The onset of 'Hitler's War' found the base prepared with anti-aircraft posts, camouflaged buildings and air-raid shelters. Control of Manston was vested in No. 11 Group of Fighter Command and much action by its aircraft ensued during the Luftwaffe attempts to subjugate the RAF fighter force in the Battle of Britain in 1940. The story of the airfield's part in this epic conflict has been often told and it is hoped that this book will pictorially complement the written accounts.

As the war progressed Manston became heavily involved in intense flying activities with virtually every type of aircraft using it either as an operational base or as a welcome refuge when lost or damaged in battle. A 3,000 yd runway, which still dominates the scene, was opened in 1944. Specifically designed to accept aircraft making crash-landings, it provided a veritable haven for many exhausted or wounded aircrew and their damaged machines. Subsequently this facility was enhanced by the introduction of FIDO, the petrol-burning system which dispersed fog and so permitted landings to be made in conditions of low or nil visibility.

The war years brought into prominence a number of services whose contributions to RAF operations and safety were most important and cannot be ignored. Radar is represented by the stations at Sandwich and Foreness. The former commenced operations in late 1943 as a fighter-control unit covering a wide area and with a range of about 100 miles. It was one of the largest, permanent Ground Controlled Interception (GCI) stations and with typical RAF humour was known in radar circles as a 'Happidrome' after a contemporary BBC comedy radio programme featuring a farcical music-hall. It closed many years ago and its place has been taken by RAF Ash, which is nearby. The Chain Home Low (CHL) station at Foreness was a trail-blazer in its fighter-control and raid-reporting roles, having operated from the earliest days of the Second World War. No trace of this historic site remains today.

The offshore raid-reporting of the RAF radar chain was complemented by the Royal Observer Corps (ROC) over the land. Staffed by 30,000 officers and observers (part and full time, male and female), the corps manned 1,400 posts in the 40 groups covering the UK. The fifty posts in Kent were undoubtedly kept at full stretch, day and night, throughout the war and none more so than those around Manston. On 24 August 1940 the extensive telephone network of the ROC proved invaluable to Manston when the bombing that continued throughout the day cut all communication with the airfield. Contact was only made possible by the gallant action of the Minster A1 Post's crew, Messrs E. Foad and P. Jezard.

The greatly increased air activity around the UK coastline during the Second World War highlighted the need for a safety service for airmen having to 'ditch' after combat. This was particularly necessary over the Channel and Thames Estuary. To meet this requirement the RAF Air/Sea Rescue (A/SR) branch was established with an eventual strength of 4,000 officers and men operating 300 launches. It is estimated that they saved no fewer than fourteen thousand lives before disbandment in April 1986. Ramsgate was the local centre for these operations which, in conjunction with A/SR aircraft, rendered vital life-saving aid to crashed or parachuted aircrew off the Kent coast.

Formed in March 1941, No. 438 (Thanet) Squadron, Air Training Corps (ATC) continues a close association with RAF Manston where its headquarters are located. Over the years the squadron has given preliminary military and aviation training to the boy and girl cadets who, whether they enter the RAF, another Service or remain in civilian life, will have benefited from their experience in the corps. On occasion, during the Second World War, the Thanet cadets' obligations and allegiance to the RAF took an unusually active form. On one occasion, they were called to the airfield to assist the servicing crews in the rearming, refuelling and making-up of ammunition belts. On another, on 12 February 1942, the lads worked on the fighters supporting the operation against the German battle-cruisers *Scharnhorst* and *Gneisnau*, and the cruiser *Prinz Eugen* escaping up the Channel. These and other chores they performed with great gusto. Almost fifty years later, in August 1990, the cadets were in annual summer camp at RAF Coltishall when the Iraquis invaded Kuwait. Their services were once again enlisted to help prepare the Jaguar aircraft destined for the Gulf War.

Following the end of hostilities the so-called 'Cold War' led to US Strategic Air Command (SAC) basing fighter bomber units at Manston, the first RAF station in the UK to be so used. A number of photographs in this selection were provided by American personnel of that period, some of whom are members of the RAF Manston History Club. Many hundreds of USAF officers and men served at the airfield between 1950 and 1958 and, despite the occasional rigours experienced, retain an affection for this corner of England which was their home for a brief time.

Shortly after the departure of the USAF the airfield became a 'joint-user', that is, it became available for both service and civilian use. Since that time there has been a continuous presence of airlines, flying-schools and maintenance firms, all located on the eastern side.

In 1961 'D' Flight No. 22 Squadron came on attachment and was quickly established as an integral part of local services with its Whirlwind search and rescue helicopters, which took part in many rescues of both service personnel and civilians. Despite strong local representations the unit was withdrawn in 1969 and Bristow Helicopters Ltd offered a civilian service. In 1974 the search and rescue unit returned in the form of 'D' Flight No. 72 Squadron and its Wessex machines, soon again to become 'E' Flight No. 22 Squadron. Finally, 1988 brought the Sea Kings of 'C' Flight No. 202 Squadron to continue the search and rescue role. The prospective loss of this much-prized local service in the near future is again causing concern. Other flying activities, related to the RAF and ATC, are those of the Air Experience Flight and the cadets' Gliding Club.

A resident organization housed in the main camp is the Defence Fire Services Central Training Establishment. The origins of air force fire-fighting and prevention go back to the First World War, when the immense growth of military flying necessitated the creation of a service dedicated to these tasks. From the early 1920s, at RAF Cranwell, the facilities have progressed from the Air Ministry Fire Service to the present-day Defence Fire Service. The training of staff similarly proceeded through such organizations as the Fire Fighting School (1922), the School of Fire Fighting and Anti-Gas (1943), the Fire and Rescue Training School (1959), up to the present Defence Fire Service's Central Training Establishment, set up in 1990. In addition to RAF firemen, civil, Royal Navy, airline, Commonwealth and foreign personnel are trained at Manston.

Such books as this and its predecessor rely wholly on material available and found by the compilers, and it is apparent that many aspects of Manston's intriguing past were not recorded photographically. However, we hope the reader will feel a reasonable and acceptable coverage has been achieved. Who knows, further photographs may yet be unearthed for a future publication.

1 PROSPECT PUB. HSE.
2 SITE OF R.N.A.S WESTGATE
3 BRITISH RAIL MARGATE
4 RAF MANSTON MAINCAMP
5 EXTENT OF ORIGINAL AIRFIELD
6 WAR FLIGHT NOW K.I.A.
7 PEGWELL HOVERPORT
8 SITE OF SUNKEN HANGAR

SECTION ONE

Earliest Beginnings: Pre-First World War

The first airman to land an aircraft in Thanet arrived on Saturday 20 April 1912. Lt. Spenser D.A. Grey with his mechanic, Fred Brown, landed in a small field adjacent to St Lawrence College, Ramsgate. They had flown from Eastchurch on the Isle of Sheppey arriving in Thanet at about 6.45 a.m. Their aircraft, a Short Biplane Type S.34, powered by a 50 hp Gnome engine, after refuelling, took off from land adjoining Newby's brickfield.

A Short biplane at Westgate, possibly S.38. Beach House can be seen in the background. This area later became part of the RNAS seaplane base at Westgate. The S.38 saw much use at the Royal Naval Air Station, Eastchurch, and it was in this type of aircraft that Lt. Samson achieved the first take-off from a ship under way, the HMS *Hibernia*, off Weymouth, on 9 May 1912.

Opposite: Sqd. Cdr. Spenser D.A. Grey in the uniform of the RNAS, during the First World War. Grey was the first airman to land in Thanet on 20 April 1912. A pioneer aviator and one of the original and most experienced pilots in the RNAS, he learned to fly in the summer of 1911 at his own expense. Later appointed to the RNAS at Eastchurch, in September 1913 he flew Winston and Mrs Churchill and later gave the former flying lessons. At the outbreak of the First World War Grey carried out bombing raids from Belgium bases on Düsseldorf and Cologne and received the DSO.

With what looks to be one of Margate's major hotels in the background, a Short biplane, possibly S.34, attracts a crowd of visitors as she sits like a great bird awaiting her pilot, Lt. C.J. L'Estrange Malone, on 30 May 1912.

The Deperdussin Monoplane 'M.1' generates much interest at Quex Park, Birchington, after landing with engine trouble on 22 April 1912 during a flight from Eastchurch. The pilot on this occasion was Lt. A.M. Longmore, destined to become Air Chief Marshal Sir Arthur Longmore.

Piloted by Mr J.L. Travers and Mr Louis Noel, this Farman 'Waterplane' showed its capabilities by giving flying exhibitions and passenger flights at Margate in August 1912 as part of the *Daily Mail* Waterplane Tour. The photo-insert shows the tour's organizer, Claude Grahame-White, owner of Hendon and promoter of its aviation meetings in the years before the First World War.

Lt. Samson at Westgate, having landed his seaplane there after developing engine trouble mid-way between Dover and Sheerness, 13 May 1912. The aircraft was a Short Type S.41 powered by a 100 hp Gnome engine, and saw much service in both landplane and seaplane forms. It was later taken in tow by HMS *Recruit* and removed to Sheerness.

Short Type S.45 (RNAS No. T.5) visiting Margate on 30 May 1912 from its base at Eastchurch. By July of that year the aircraft had been fitted with floats, later reverting to a wheeled undercarriage for the army manœuvres of autumn 1912. The aircraft later saw service as a floatplane until struck off charge after it capsized in October 1912.

Another view of Short Biplane S.45 on 30 May 1912. Lt. Spenser Grey is inspecting the 70 hp Gnome engine while Lt. Sheppard makes his way to the rear of the aircraft. On the left, standing in front of Lt. Sheppard, is Lt. Malone and next to him the Mayor of Margate, Alderman Adutt. The aircraft was later flown back to Eastchurch.

Claude Grahame-White, organizer of the *Daily Mail*-sponsored Waterplane Tour, which took place in the summer of 1912. The aircraft visited Margate and were seen by thousands of visitors when at anchor off the Winter Gardens. The photograph captures the spirit of early flying and, clearly, no self-respecting pioneer would take off without the correct 'flying-clothing', including the neat bow-tie.

Mr Cecil Grace, pioneer aviator and the first instructor for the early RNAS pilots at Eastchurch, disappeared after leaving Calais while competing for the Baron de Forest Prize on 22 December 1912. Flying a Short S.27 powered by a 60 hp ENV engine, he was last heard passing over a Ramsgate fishing smack, the *San Toy*.

M. Manio arrived in his Bleriot monoplane in a field adjacent to George Hill Coastguard Station, Kingsgate, on Sunday 2 December 1912. He had flown over from Boulogne with his dog, Jim, who wisely decided to stay in Kingsgate when Manio took off only to crash later on to the roof of a house in Palmers Green, London.

Henri Salmet's aircraft, a Bleriot monoplane, on land lent by the local council at Cliftonville, Margate, in August 1913. In two hours Salmet took up nine passengers, the event being sponsored by the *Daily Mail*. It is perhaps no coincidence that the owner of the *Daily Mail*, Lord Northcliffe, lived nearby in Reading Street.

Salmet first arrived in Thanet on 13 August 1912 having flown from Gravesend. He was engaged by the *Daily Mail* to give displays nation-wide and in Thanet operated from a field, near the power-station at St Peters, which at that time formed part of Callis Grange Farm.

Ramsgate was chosen as the first control point for the *Daily Mail* £5,000 Round Britain Seaplane Race. The first competitor to arrive, Harry Hawker flying a Sopwith seaplane, landed outside the harbour on 16 August 1913. The then Mayor of Ramsgate, Alderman Gwyn, presented Hawker with a silver trophy at a ceremony held at the Pavilion.

Harry Hawker's Sopwith seaplane outside Ramsgate Harbour after landing to check in at the control point. This was the only aircraft of the original entrants to start the Circuit of Britain Race. Unfortunately Hawker had to retire through illness at Yarmouth.

A striking shot of a Short Pusher Seaplane (possibly S.79) powered by a 100 hp Gnome Monosoupape engine taking off from Ramsgate in early 1914. The old fish-dock forms the backdrop. Owned by Frank McClean, the aircraft was later taken into Government service but was completely wrecked in August 1915.

Short's 'Gun-Carrying' Seaplane S.81 (RNAS No. 126), powered by a 160 hp Gnome engine, at Ramsgate in August 1914 after being damaged by rough weather. The aircraft was later dismantled and returned by road to Sheerness. The S.81 carried a 1½ pdr Vickers quick-firing gun but was later fitted with an up-rated 6 pdr Davis Gun for trials on the Isle of Grain.

SECTION TWO

The First World War

In the years 1915 to 1918 the German naval airships' bombing campaign against England and especially the south-east was not without losses. The Zeppelin L.15 is shown wrecked off Margate after being hit by anti-aircraft gunfire near Purfleet on the night of 31 March 1916.

In an attempt to combat the German attacks, the Royal Flying Corps and the Royal Naval Air Service flew defensive patrols on receipt of warning of the approach of raiders. Operating from Manston, this BE2c aircraft of the latter service took part in many such sorties as a machine of the War Flight.

The transfer of the landplanes from Westgate to Manston in 1916 necessitated the construction of suitable hangarage at the new base. To meet this need an original Westgate hangar was removed and re-erected on the present Kent International Airport site. It was finally demolished in 1989.

The ex-Westgate hangar in the later years of its service at Manston in 1975. As well as other uses, it at one time housed the gliders of the Air Training Corps cadets. The design was a standard one, more widely seen on RFC aerodromes than those of the RNAS.

The original living-quarters for officers and men located in the East Camp or War Flight as it was called in the First World War, 1916. The road in the foreground, 'Coke Alley', was situated behind the hangars. The apparent patches on the roofs were a camouflage measure of the time. These huts were still extant in the 1950s.

Handley Page Type O/100 (No. 1456) was the second prototype of a line of very successful heavy bombers in the First World War. Arriving at Manston in July 1916 it joined the then forming Handley Page Squadron, with which it served until October 1917 mainly in a training role. On 1 August 1916 it flew – most unusually – a defensive sortie during a Zeppelin raid.

Officers of No. 3 Wing, RNAS, on arrival in France. The officers were mostly ex-Manston, where the unit was formed in 1916, its function being the bombing of industrial targets in the Saar. The CO, Wg. Cdr. W.L. Elder (left) is seated by Sqn. Cdr. R.B. Davies VC, and second from the left is Flt. Sub-Lt. R. Collishaw, destined to become a famous fighter pilot on the Western Front.

One of the Sopwith 1½ Strutter aircraft of No. 3 Wing in collision with a Ford car on the road which crosses the aerodrome. They manage things differently now and, with the aid of traffic lights, barriers and loud-hailers, keep airborne vehicles separated from those on the ground. In this case everyone had a laugh – except the insurance company.

Light-hearted RNAS officers, possibly pilots of the War Flight or No. 3 Wing, fooling about with the Manston steam-roller in the summer of 1916. Unfortunately the men are unidentified, though the officer on the extreme right looks remarkably like Flt. Lt. (at that time) Chris Draper, later called the 'Mad Major', famous for flying under bridges.

On the night of 16/17 June 1917 two Zeppelin airships, L.42 and L.48, were en route to attack London when weather and engine trouble caused a change of target, L.42 bombing Ramsgate instead. The young lady is holding a souvenir of the raid, apparently a small bomb or similar object which fell from the airship.

Albert Street, Ramsgate, which suffered extensive damage as a result of the Zepplin raid at 0200 hours on 17 June 1917. Three people were killed, sixteen injured and damage was caused to the value of £28,159. A massive explosion shook the town following a direct hit on a naval ammunition store by a 600 lb bomb.

A Nieuport Type XI Scout calling in at Manston on 14 September 1916 and clearly arousing the curiosity of those present. Situated as it was in an area of much flying activity, Manston received its share of visiting aircraft from neighbouring aerodromes or those in transit and this was a typical example.

Sent to Manston in February 1917, this Hispano-Suiza-engined Sopwith Triplane joined the War Flight for evaluation under operational conditions. Although it flew a number of Home Defence sorties it was not put into production. This first prototype, N.509, was finally crashed on 29 October 1917 by Flt. Lt. A.F. Brandon.

The Manston War Flight flew a variety of aircraft between 1916 and 1918 but BE and Bristol Scout types predominated. This line-up of the latter was typical of the early 1917 period. N5392, first on the right, engaged in many Home Defence flights from April 1917 until March 1918 when it was crashed near Sandwich.

This Handley Page bomber (No. 3126) had a busy existence from its introduction into RNAS service in 1916 until February 1918 when it crashed in France after a bombing operation. The bizarre marking is associated with camouflage experiments in which it participated. The plane visited Manston briefly on three occasions.

An artist's impression of one of the ten twin-engined Gotha bombers which attacked Margate, Ramsgate and Dover from their bases near Ghent on 22 August 1917. As a result of the raid, twelve people were killed and twenty-seven injured. Three of the raiders were destroyed, this one brought down by local anti-aircraft gun batteries and crashing at Vincent's Farm.

One of the long-serving Bristol Scout aircraft of the War Flight, N5398 made a number of flights against the German raiders from January 1917 to August of that year when it was retired to a training role with the War School, where it was crashed on 16 August 1917.

Among its other chores Manston occasionally carried out service tests on new aircraft, such as this Armstrong Whitworth FK.10, numbered N511. Intended as a two-seater fighter its quadruplane wing layout was one of the unique designs of Dutchman Fredk. Koolhoven. It did not go into production.

This highly decorated Sopwith Camel (B3926) was probably the mount of an instructor of the Pilots Pool, Manston, in 1918. It had earlier served with the War Flight for a short time and later went to the flying school at Redcar. The starboard side fuselage carried the inscription 'Happy Hawkins'.

Avro 504C, No. 1485, was a training aircraft of the War School from May to the end of August 1917 when it was wrecked on landing by Flt. Lt. R.E. Darnton. This type of mishap was commonplace at flying schools, though usually without death or serious injury resulting.

In contrast to the previous incident, the pilot of this Sopwith Camel B5734 of the War School, 18-year-old Flt. Sub-Lt. W.N. Cross, was killed on 6 March 1918. Along with several other airmen who lost their lives at or near Manston, Cross is buried in Minster cemetery.

Ground crew members of No. 219 Squadron, Manston, with a DH.9 aircraft of the unit. Probably taken in late 1918 the photo shows the mixed nature of the personnel – ex-RFC and RNAS – to be found in all units of the RAF and who continued to wear the uniform of their original service.

DH.4, B9486, first saw service as an advanced training aircraft with the DH.4 School of the RNAS in January 1918. Subsequently it was flown by Nos 203 and 55 Training Depot Stations (TDS), the successive, large training units at Manston, until almost the end of the First World War. Although designed in early 1916 the DH.4 remained a high-performance aircraft.

A group of pupil pilots with their instructor during the course at No. 203 TDS, Manston, June 1918. The aircraft is a BE2c, a widely used training machine. From left to right: Mason, -?-, Stow, Fleischer, Scott, Moulson, Wickham (on the ground). Their uniforms confirm them as originally RFC cadets although they are now in the RAF.

Cadet Wickham ready for flight in a DH.6 of No. 203 TDS, Manston. Note the combined cockpit, the voice-tube for instructor/pupil communication, the gravity fuel tank below the upper wing and the brass, basic ignition switch. This elementary training machine was wryly known as 'The Clutching Hand' or 'The Dung Hunter'.

An early stage in the excavations in preparation for the first of the sunken hangars at Alland Grange in 1918. The spoil removed was deposited along the sides of the 'hole' and was largely chalk. The machinery used makes an interesting contrast with the equipment which would be utilized today.

Experiments to obtain early warning of the positions of raiding aircraft were carried out in the First World War using fixed or adjustable sound mirrors on the Kent coastline. Illustrated is the equipment of one such investigation on the Joss Bay cliff in 1918. Aircraft from Manston flew for some of the tests, which were only partially successful.

The Twenties and Thirties

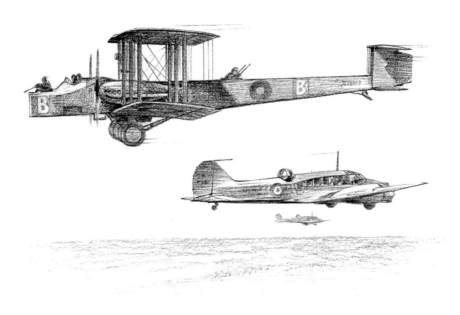

Avro 504K, G–EAJQ, awaiting the first customers of the season, *c.* 1921. This particular aircraft, built in Manchester in 1919, attended the first Air Traffic Exhibition at Amsterdam in August of that year. Powered by a Clerget 130 hp engine the 504K was used extensively for pleasure trips during the 1920s and '30s.

The Avro 504K in military guise. E3798 was one of a batch of 500 built by Avro's during the First World War. This particular aircraft was used as a 'hack' or training machine by No. 9 Squadron when based at Manston in the early twenties.

Opposite: Capt. D. Milner Deighton at Margate in 1919. Deighton was an ex-instructor at the famous Gosport School of Special Flying where systematic flying training was first developed by Major R.R. Smith-Barry. The Avro 504 was used to give pleasure trips during the summer season and proved very popular with the visitors.

An excellent and detailed view of an Avro 504K with ground crew in attendance, during the early 1920s at Manston. Note the drip-tray placed under the aircraft to catch oil from the notoriously dirty rotary engine.

Airmen in their barrack room at Manston during the 1920s. It is interesting to note the old pattern uniform with its high dog-collar tunic fastened at the neck. The only heat within the barrack room came from a coke stove, which gives the impression that this particular photograph was taken in the depths of winter.

A postcard view of Manston dating from 1926. This particular card was posted to a Mrs Taylor of Sandwich and stated that the sender would be pleased to see her on the following Sunday. The view takes in most of the airfield, looking east along the road that cuts across the main grass.

Vickers Virginia J8239 of No. 9 Squadron after a crash-landing. The Virginia had been in collision with a Bristol F2B Fighter (J7666) of No. 2 Squadron over Manston on 14 March 1928. The two officers in the Bristol lost their lives. The pilot of the Virginia managed to crash-land in a field adjacent to the aerodrome.

'Armed to the teeth'. Vickers Virginia J6856 complete with 'fighting tops' in flight over Manston in 1927. As an experiment gunners' cockpits had been fitted in the top mainplane. Powered by 500 hp Napier Lion engines, J6856 saw service with No. 7 and No. 215 Squadrons before being struck off charge in 1937.

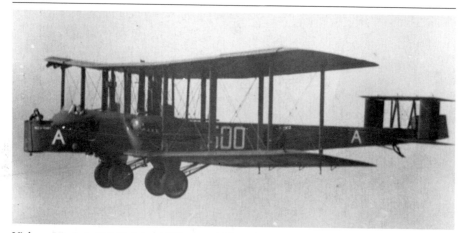

Vickers Virginia J8240 *Isle of Thanet* of No. 500 Squadron, based at Manston, 1931. On 4 June 1931 the aircraft was 'christened' with Kentish cider during a ceremony carried out by the then Mayor of Ramsgate, Alderman Terry. While serving with No. 7 Squadron the aircraft was badly damaged in a forced-landing at Sevenoaks but was later rebuilt as an Mk.IX.

Air and ground crew stand in front of Virginia J8240 'A' of No. 500 Squadron. The squadron, manned by half regular and half reserve personnel, suffered the fate of all Royal Auxiliary Air Force squadrons, being disbanded in March 1957. No. 500 Squadron had a strong connection with RAF Manston having been formed there as a Special Reserve Unit in March 1931.

An aerial view of Manston Main Camp, 1933. The aircraft in front of the hangar belong to No. 2 (Army Co-operation) Squadron. At that time the unit flew the Armstrong Whitworth Atlas, re-equipping with the Hawker Audax in May 1933.

Westland Wapiti IIa's of No. 608 Squadron visiting RAF Manston during the mid-1930s. The squadron was based at Thornaby and operated as a day-bomber unit of the Auxiliary Air Force.

Members of No. 2 (AC) Squadron in front of their Hawker Audax aircraft during their 1934 annual summer camp. That year saw them 'roughing it' at Friday Street, near Colchester, Essex. (The Army just had to get into the picture with their Vickers Tank.) No. 2 Squadron operated the Audax in the Army Co-operation role for nearly three years, finally re-equipping with the Hawker Hector. Today the squadron operates the multi-role Jaguar.

The carpenter's workshop in the mid-1930s, part of the School of Technical Training at RAF Manston. The syllabus within the school comprised a variety of trades and skills. All subjects taught led to a high degree of skill, needed to service the aircraft of the period.

Avro Prefect K5066 at RAF Manston while serving with the School of Air Navigation, later No. 48 Squadron. One of seven Prefects delivered in June and July 1935, K5066 was sold in May 1946 and operated on the civil market as G–AHVO.

The family of Hawker biplanes are without question some of the most beautiful aircraft ever to grace the sky. Hawker Hart K4459 served with No. 500 Squadron at RAF Manston during the mid-1930s. This particular aircraft was part of a batch built by Armstrong Whitworth and delivered between January and May 1935.

A formation fly-past by Avro Ansons of the School of Air Navigation in 1937, during practice for the Empire Air Day. The photograph was taken from the top-turret of the leading machine. The Anson served with the RAF up until the early 1960s.

Avro Ansons of the School of Air Navigation in formation over Manston, *c.* 1936. The Anson was the first aircraft in RAF service with a retractable undercarriage. No. 48 Squadron, based at Manston, took delivery of the Anson Mk.I in March 1936.

The ubiquitous Avro 504N, J8761. This particular aircraft served with Nos 2 and 9 Squadrons and finally, in 1931, the Oxford University Air Squadron, thus spending its entire service life at RAF Manston.

A good air-to-air shot of Avro 504N, K2412, over Manston during the mid-1930s. It was one of two of the type serving with No. 500 Squadron during this period.

Personnel of No. 9 (Bomber) Squadron in front of one of the main hangars at Manston in 1924. The aircraft are, from left to right: Avro 504K, Vickers Vimy, Sopwith Snipe and a Bristol Fighter. The squadron was equipped with Vimys from April 1924 to June 1925.

SECTION FOUR
Hitler's War

Minster Section, the Observer Corps, just after the outbreak of war in 1939. Later in the conflict uniforms were issued to the personnel (see p. 124). The Minster Section manned the posts adjacent to RAF Manston. Back row, left to right: Icke Horne, E. Chase (Landlord of The Bell, Minster), Bill Sackett, Ern Lucas, Jack White. Second row: Bill Petts, Norman Smith, Ted Young, Peter Young, Jack Player, Ted Foad, Percy Golder. Front row: -?-, Bill Slaughter.

Percy Golder of the Minster Section manning the post adjacent to the airfield. The device on the small plotting table is a Micklethwaite Height Correction Attachment, a very important piece of equipment which gave the height of enemy aircraft. The wall-chart was used for aircraft recognition, detailing both British and enemy machines.

The remains of No. 4 Gun Post after the Luftwaffe attack on 24 August 1940. This raid was one of the heaviest carried out by the Germans during the Battle of Britain period. Twenty enemy bombers attacked the airfield which brought a sharp response from the ground defences. Seven men died and the damage to the airfield was considerable.

A Light Anti-Aircraft gun, possibly a 20 mm cannon. Prior to the introduction of the 40 mm Bofors, the air defence of RAF Manston in 1940 rested with these light weapons. If anything, at least they could deter low-flying enemy aircraft. The 'erk' with his arm resting on the breach is Bill Brown. Perhaps the photograph was taken during 'stand-down' or a quiet period between raids. (An 'erk' was the general term used to denote all those unfortunates below the rank of corporal.)

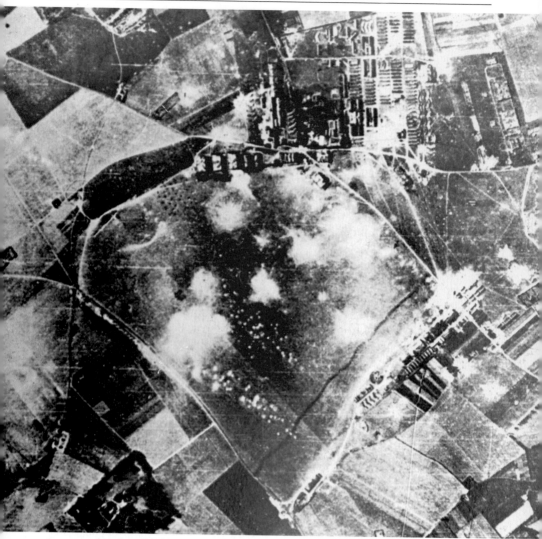

A captured Luftwaffe photograph depicting a raid on RAF Manston. This could well be the raid of 24 August 1940. The area was littered with craters and unexploded bombs. Communications had been cut leaving the station all but isolated.

Opposite: Fritz Buchner died when his Messerschmitt Bf 109E–1 crashed on Shuart's Marshes not far from St Nicholas at Wade on Monday 26 August 1940. Shot down by FO K.J. Marston of No. 56 Squadron, Buchner's body lay for many years buried deep in the Kentish clay. The wreckage and the young pilot's remains were excavated in 1984 and after a lengthy investigation Fritz Buchner was finally laid to rest in 1986, forty-six years after his last combat.

Spitfires of No. 92 Squadron take off from Manston in early February 1941. The squadron was one of the highest scoring units in the Battle of Britain. Their stay at Manston was fairly brief, being of only two months, and at the end of February they moved to Biggin Hill.

Members of No. 92 Squadron scramble. While serving at Manston the squadron was credited with shooting down the last Ju 87 (Stuka) to fall on British soil, on 5 February 1941. The Ju 87 had just attacked HM Trawler *Tourmaline* in mid-Channel. It was on the outskirts of the airfield that Plt. Off. R.H. Fokes of No. 92 Squadron shot down the German dive-bomber, which crashed at 9.50 a.m. killing its two-man crew.

A typical wartime Air Training Corps (ATC) cadet, George Bolton, aged 17, from Ramsgate. Note the old style tunic buttoned to the neck. Many young boys such as George later served with the Royal Air Force during the Second World War.

Fifty years on and past members of No. 438 (Thanet) Squadron ATC hold a memorial service on 21 April 1991 at Holy Trinity church, Northdown, Margate.

No. 438 (Thanet) Squadron (ATC) at Chatham House School, Ramsgate, 1942. During RAF operations from Manston, boys from the corps would help rearm and refuel aircraft, giving them a first-hand insight into life at a forward fighter station. A number of these young boys would later give their lives in the service of their country. No. 438 was formed in 1941.

Flt. Lt. Richard Playne Stevens DSO, DFC and Bar, a pre-war commercial pilot who became one of the first 'intruders' of note, operating from RAF Manston. Flying over Luftwaffe bases in France and Belgium he would attack any German aircraft or target of opportunity. He lost his life in December 1941 during a sortie to a German airfield in Holland.

Members of No. 174 'Mauritius' Squadron, Manston, 1942. Back row, left to right: Plt. Off. Hallett, Sgt. Seely, Sgt. James, Flt. Lt. McPhail, Flt. Lt. McConnel DFC, Plt. Off. Robinson. Front row, Flt. Sgt. Wettere, Flt. Sgt. Montgomery and Sgt. Tye. The squadron had been formed at Manston on 3 March 1942 from a nucleus of No. 607 Squadron.

Fleet Air Arm pilots from No. 841 Squadron leave their Albacore after a successful mission against enemy shipping. Lt. Walsh (left) and Sub-Lt. Patrick stand-down for a well-deserved rest at Manston, 1943.

Sub-Lt. Patrick and Lt. Walsh, preparing for yet another mission, confirm the target with the squadron's Intelligence Officer. No. 841 Squadron was finally disbanded at Manston on 1 December 1943.

Flt. Sgt. John Brooks of No. 174 Squadron in his Hurricane, Manston, March 1942. The squadron carried out fighter-bomber missions mainly against enemy shipping, later handing over their Hurricanes for the new Hawker Typhoons.

Members of No. 137 Squadron with their CO in front of their Westland Whirlwinds at RAF Manston in 1943. Powered by two Rolls-Royce Peregrine Mk.I engines, the Whirlwind proved a formidable ground-attack aircraft.

'R' Robert, Boston IIIa, of No. 88 Squadron, crossing the Channel in low-level formation with companions. On 22 October 1943 this aircraft returned from operations with its starboard engine burned out and landed at Manston having been escorted back by Typhoons of No. 3 Squadron, based at the airfield.

'R' Robert and pilot, Jack Peppiatt, who is the present co-chairman of RAF Manston History Club. The observer is Sid Kirk who was killed in Tunisia in 1943.

The grave of Flt. Lt. 'The Baron' Jean De Selys Longchamps DFC of No. 3 Squadron in Minster cemetery. The Baron, a second cousin of the King of Belgium and famous for his single-handed attack on the Gestapo HQ in Brussels, died while attempting a night landing in his Typhoon EJ950 on 15 August 1943.

An aerial view of RAF Sandwich Radar Station during the Second World War. One of the largest type GCIs in the Second World War, it came into operation in 1943 replacing both Willesborough (Kent) and Foulness (Essex). This type of Ground Control Interception station was facetiously known as a 'Happidrome'.

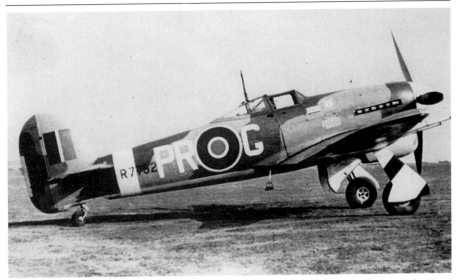

Hawker Typhoon R7752, personalized with the victory scoreboard of Sqn. Ldr. 'Bee' Beamont, of No. 609 'West Riding' Squadron operating from RAF Manston in mid-1943.

A group of WAAFs at RAF Manston, *c.* 1943. The WAAFs were the very backbone of the RAF and the maids of all work. The WAAF reached a wartime peak of 6,000 officers and 176,000 other ranks. Mrs Marjorie Everest, centre front, provided this photograph.

Members of No. 198 Squadron at Manston, January 1944. Among those present are: FO H. Freeman, FO J.F.H. Williams, FO Rainsforth, Flt. Sgt. J.S. Fraser-Petherbridge, WO J. Allan, Flt. Lt. J.W. Scrambler, Flt. Lt. D. Sweeting, WO H.A. Hallett, Flt. Lt. P.D. Roper, Flt. Lt. R.J. Dall, FO W. Parkes, WO G.J. Stokes, Flt. Lt. J. Niblett, FO W.G. Eagle, Flt. Sgt. R.C.A. Crouch, Sgt. J.S. Madgett, Flt. Lt. J.M. Plamondon, Flt. Lt. R.A. Lallemant.

Two WAAFs of the MT Section, RAF Manston, *c.* 1943. The Fordson tractor was the means of moving aircraft and the petrol bowsers round the airfield. The lady on the left is now Mrs Dorothy Daniel.

SECTION FIVE

Post-Second World War

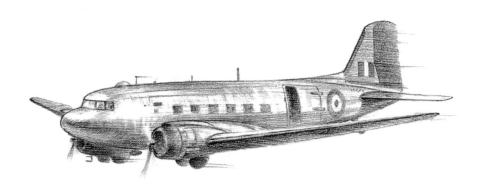

Members of No. 77 Squadron at Manston in the summer of 1947 during Exercise Longstop. The squadron's role was to drop members of the Parachute Regiment on to pre-selected 'drop-zones'. The squadron was based at RAF Manston from September 1947 to November 1948. The unit took an active part in the Berlin Airlift, flying Dakota aircraft.

Air Marshal Sir Dermot A. Boyle KVCO, Air Officer Commanding Fighter Command, arrives at RAF Manston to carry out the annual AOC's inspection, 1955. He is being met by Grp. Capt. E.S. Finch, Sqn. Ldr. A. Lloyd DFC, Flt. Lt. J. Saunders RAFO and the Revd F. Gower Smith of Monkton.

A member of the famous Russian Bolshoi Ballet company is given a helping hand from one of the three TU 104s that landed on the airfield on 1 October 1956. The troupe of dancers later made their way to London by coach, the aircraft having been diverted to Manston because of inclement weather.

A view from the Silver City hangar with two Hermes airliners parked on the tarmac. The photograph dates from 1959: it was in that year that four Hermes were transferred to Manston. The site now adjoins the Kent International Airport complex.

Canberra WE168, a P.R.3 version of this famous jet-bomber, is edged into position after arrival from 231 OCU (Operational Conversation Unit). The aircraft served with Nos 540, 69 and 39 Squadrons, being struck off charge on 13 May 1969. The Canberra was a familiar sight at Manston but finally ended its days on the Fire Fighting School dump. The Spitfire stands on what is now part of the Spitfire and Hurricane Museum.

The Freedom of Sandwich is granted to RAF Sandwich on 3 July 1955. A detachment of WAAFs salute the Mayor of Sandwich outside the Guild Hall, giving a snappy 'eyes left' as they march through the old town.

The 'Luftwaffe' arrive at RAF Manston on Saturday 11 May 1968 to take part in the feature film *The Battle of Britain*. The aircraft flew in from Spain and close inspection reveals that the He111 bombers are in fact CASA 2.111s powered by Rolls-Royce Merlins. Wg. Cdr. 'Bob' Stanford Tuck was on hand to greet this unlikely armada, having had first-hand experience in attacking the real thing over Kent twenty-eight years earlier.

Members of the Italian 'Frecce Tricolori' in front of one of the team's Fiat G.91 jet-fighters during a visit to RAF Manston in September 1969. The Italians took Europe by storm with their high standard of 'display' flying, a standard the Red Arrows would later exhibit not only in Europe but throughout the world.

Visitors cast an 'expert eye' over one of the Manston Gliding School craft at one of RAF Manston's many open days. Young ATC cadets received their first taste of flying with the gliding school.

Air Vice-Marshal Clementi, with Wg. Cdr. Scott in attendance, takes a keen interest in the operation of the Air Traffic Control when visiting the Control Tower. The Air Vice-Marshal had been to the station on a previous occasion to present a Commendation to Cpl. McEvoy, who had been instrumental in setting up various sporting activities on the station.

An aerial view of the Manston Control Tower, 1970s. The tower has seen many changes both externally and internally, although alterations to the building over the years have not changed the general shape of the structure. However, if one examines a present-day photograph closely, changes can be seen.

At first sight one would think this was a wartime photograph. Actually it was taken in the summer of 1973 when a visiting Hurricane dropped in. The personnel standing round the aircraft are, in fact, ATC lads casting an appreciative eye over this famous Second World War fighter.

A visiting Spitfire receives rapt attention from the youngsters during a flying visit in 1980. To add to the crowd's delight, the 'stunt stand-ins' from the feature film *The Empire Strikes Back* put in an appearance as well.

WD331, a De Havilland Chipmunk of No. 1 Air Experience Flight, at RAF Manston. The arrival of the first Chipmunk at Manston in 1968 enabled the local ATC cadets to gain 'powered-flight' experience. The first Chipmunk flew in 1946 having been designed in Canada. Powered by a Gipsy Major engine the aircraft has a top speed of 138 mph.

Flown by a member of the local air cadets, a glider from No. 617 Gliding School comes in to land at Manston. The school moved from Bovingdon to Manston in late 1970.

T.G. Aviation's hangar and clubhouse, which stand close to the eastern end of the runway. In 1983 Ted Girdler, a former Red Arrows pilot, set up his charter, aircraft hire and pilot training flying club. This family-run aviation business retains close links with the RAF presence at Manston.

THIS MEMORIAL
WAS ERECTED IN SEPTEMBER 1990
TO MARK THE FIFTIETH ANNIVERSARY OF
THE BATTLE OF BRITAIN
IN HONOUR OF
THOSE WHO DIED AND FOUGHT
FOR THEIR COUNTRY
AND TO COMMEMORATE
ALL THE PEOPLE OF THANET
WHO ENDURED THE CONFLICT

A simple memorial located outside the Spitfire and Hurricane Museum at Manston to mark the fiftieth anniversary of the Battle of Britain and to honour all those who fought and died for a freedom we take so much for granted today.

SECTION SIX
USAF at Manston

Manston, February 1952. Before the wooden barracks were constructed American Air Force personnel lived in tents. Canvas hung over a wooden frame with a wooden floor became a home from home for two years. Airman Bernard 'Shag' Shaughnessey stands in front of 'Tent City' on what is now part of the Spitfire and Hurricane Museum complex.

Manston's mobile snack-bar, December 1952. Hot coffee and doughnuts provided a welcome respite to those chill December winds cutting across the airfield.

The scene after an F–84
Thunderjet smashed into a field
near Deal, Kent, following engine
failure on 24 August 1952. Note
the Coles Crane used to remove
what remains of the aircraft.

Known as the 'Boxcar' or 'Packet', the Fairchild C–119 saw service not only in Europe
but also Korea. Robust and ideally suited to operating from rough airstrips, these
aircraft served the USAF for many years, ending their service in the early 1970s.

Early December and a Boeing calls to refuel. Occasionally aircraft such as this B-29 would drop in, which gave all those 1950s aviation buffs a real treat. In RAF service the B-29 was known as the 'Washington'.

'Life ain't easy, brother.' A fatigue party gets ready to clean and wax the floor in the Radio Repair Shop. Like all forms of service life, duties sometimes came down to what could be termed 'routine'.

An F–84 Thunderjet manufactured by the Republic Aviation Corporation wings its way across European skies. The variant in service with the 20th Fighter Bomber Wing, the F–84E, saw active service in Korea.

Sgt. Bayne of the 123rd Maintenance Squadron outside the Radio Repair Shop during the winter of 1952. Trying to keep warm through those cold English winters meant there was never a dull moment. The bucket of coke and the shovel tell their own story.

Looking into the shark's mouth – the air-intake of an F–86, May 1953. The F–86 'Sabre' first flew in 1947 as a single-seat fighter-bomber. The 406th Fighter Bomber Group based at Manston were re-equipped with the F–86F and the unit was redesignated the 406th Fighter Interceptor Squadron.

USAF personnel 'putting their backs into it', making their own 'sidewalk', 1953. A late September sun makes the task less arduous. These 'guys' will no doubt be looking forward to an evening at The Crown or Good Intent, two of Margate's pubs with warm welcomes.

The hangar on the right, which is still extant, was used by the 514th Fighter Bomber Squadron, that on the left by the Maintenance Squadron and the low, central building was that unit's Orderly Room. This housed the Squadron Commander's and other offices in which the paperwork was handled and personnel records were kept.

Another 'Alert' during August 1953. With helmets, side-arms and carbine these two NCOs are just about ready for anything. One thing you could say about serving at Manston is that life was never dull.

'This is me, Mother.' The boys outside their beloved tent. Back row, left to right: Thompson, Easley, Kaehlen, Merriell, Wilson. Front row: Haare, Kent, -?-. According to the caption on the back of this photograph, 'we all lived in this tent from 1951 to 1953'.

An F–86 single-seat interceptor, 113509, sits on the hard standing at Manston in August 1953. This particular aircraft served with the 514th Fighter Bomber Squadron and was fated to crash on 3 December 1953 killing its pilot, Capt. Burrows.

The 406th Air Police Squadron on parade, Manston, 1955. It is interesting to note that a detachment of USAF Military Police was also based at Ramsgate and Margate civil police stations (to keep wayward airman on the straight and narrow, no doubt).

T/Sgt. Malcotte and M/Sgt. Vannekovan with the 514th Fighter Interceptor Squadron mascot, 'Russell' the goat, Manston, 1955. One wonders what became of Russell – retirement on a local farm perhaps?

The crew-chief makes one last check before take-off. The aircraft is a T–33 manufactured by Lockheed. These aircraft were based at Manston to train pilots in the fighter-bomber role.

Entering into the yule-tide spirit, Santa grabs a ride in an A/SR helicopter. It is Christmas 1955 and Flt. Lt. G. Rideout (on the left) and Sqn. Ldr. P.A. Alt (with his young son) provide an escort for dear old Santa. It should be remembered that the American service men at Manston spent a lot of time and effort making life a little bit brighter for some of the less well-off youngsters in Thanet.

Grp. Capt. Gordon Oldbury, the Commanding Officer of RAF Manston, inspects the station, December 1955. USAF personnel man the Control Tower and carry on with their air traffic control duties. The young officer on the extreme left of the photograph looks as if Christmas could not come soon enough.

The Orderly Room personnel together with the crane crew, Manston, 1955. The 'Lorain' could lift loads in the region of 6 to 8 tons. One has to ask how they all got down again.

A view of the Control Tower during the mid-1950s. As on all airfields the tower is the focal point of all air movements. Compare its appearance with that of fifteen years later (p. 82).

An informal shot of Col.
Manson (left), officer
commanding USAF personnel at
Manston, and Grp. Capt.
Oldbury (centre), commanding
the station, December 1955.

The final parade as the American personnel march towards their barracks for the last time on 30 June 1958. Eight years service came to an end as the various units and squadrons were distributed to other bases both within the UK and in Europe.

An F–84 Thunderjet rests outside the 512th Fighter Bomber Squadron hangar at Manston, *c.* 1957–8. The 512th together with the 513th and 514th, all part of the 406th Fighter Bomber Group, were assigned to 3rd Air Force. This hangar, located on the Loop, still exists at the western end of the airfield.

The slogan on the sign outside the 512th Fighter Bomber Squadron hangar says it all – 'Pride Of The 406th F.B. Grp. Envy Of The 513th and 514th F.B. Sq. Justification For The 406th'. The photograph was taken in mid-1958 and it would not be long before all this unit's pride was but a memory as Manston said farewell to the USAF later that year. To some it was the end of an era. . . .

SECTION SEVEN

Lifeline Manston

An Albion vehicle in use as an ambulance at Manston, *c.* 1937. Having first been used in 1914, Albion vehicles were for a long time associated with the British air services. One model for the RAF, the Type AM.463 chassis, proved to be particularly versatile and saw use as fire-engines, petrol bowsers, general-purpose tenders and mobile dental surgeries as well as ambulances.

With the large-scale use of float planes and flying-boats by the RNAS and RAF in the First World War a need for motor-boat tenders arose, their function being to assist in handling these aircraft when water-borne or to give aid when circumstances caused forced landings at sea. RAF.959 was one of those in use at Westgate in 1918.

ML.123, an armed motor-launch designed for RN use, against the harbour wall at Ramsgate, where it was based, in 1918. Larger and faster than RAF seaplane tenders, it could operate in liaison with Westgate's machines in more distant offshore areas due to its superior seagoing qualities.

The small amount of space below, all that was permitted by the 63 ft length and 17 ft beam of the standard Air/Sea Rescue launch, was reminiscent of a submarine. Looking forward, the navigator is seen at work in the 'chartroom' with the circular mounting of a gun-turret beyond and above. It was said that 'Whaleback' rides were better recalled than remembered!

Originally crews of Second World War Air/Sea Rescue boats preferred not to carry armament as life-saving was their concern. However, two launches were sunk by German attacks in August 1941 so machine-gun turrets were then fitted. Three more boats and twenty crew were lost at Dieppe in August 1942 and thereafter 20 mm Oerliken cannons were carried.

Personnel of the Air/Sea Rescue service based at Ramsgate Harbour, *c.* 1943. The launches normally carried a nine-man crew comprising the skipper (a commissioned officer), first- and second-class coxswains, two deckhands, two engineers, a W/T operator and a medical orderly. Clothing was an assortment of oilskins, sou'westers, roll-neck pullovers, flak-jackets and Mae Wests.

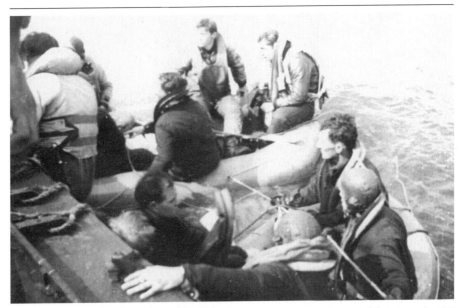

A USAF Flying Fortress crew which had 'ditched' are picked up safely. Launch 189 from Ramsgate was called on to retrieve these flyers who, apparently, had quite efficiently carried out their 'ditching drill' by launching the Fortress's own inflatable dinghies and boarding them. They are about to join No. 189.

A/SR launch 149, Ramsgate, pulls alongside a relieved Plt. Off. Reynolds on 20 May 1942. He had bailed out 18 miles east of South Foreland but carried out the 'drill' in exemplary fashion – got rid of his parachute, inflated his dinghy and Mae West and erected his radio mast complete with flag. A perfect pick-up.

The increasingly aggressive actions of the enemy air and sea forces towards the A/SR launches resulted in the introduction of heavier armament. Twin Lewis machine-guns were fitted at the stern plus a single Lewis in each turret. At a later date Browning guns replaced the Lewis and an Oerliken cannon was added.

No. 127, with its turrets and Oerliken cannon, was typical of the more heavily armed 'Whaleback' class of A/SR launch. This boat served at Calshot, Dover and Ramsgate in the period June 1941 to May 1946 until damaged in a collision. Here it is departing from Ramsgate at low tide.

The most commonly used Air/Sea Rescue launches were the 'Whaleback' and 'Hants and Dorset' classes, No. 149 being one of the sixty-five of the former type. This boat had a long period of service from August 1941 to May 1957.

In spite of much local opposition the SAR helicopter coverage by the detached Flight of No. 22 Squadron at Manston was withdrawn in March 1969. After more than two years its place was taken by the civilian Bristow Helicopters Ltd who began their contract in June 1971. Illustrated is one of their two silver and orange coloured Whirlwind machines operated on behalf of HM Coastguard until the return of the RAF in October 1974.

Two Westland Wessex HAR.2 helicopters of 'E' Flight, No. 22 Squadron, display themselves before the Manston Control Tower in the late 1970s. The Wessex, powered by two Bristol Siddeley Gnome engines, saw much use in the search and rescue role around the UK in the hands of Flights of Nos 22 and 72 Squadrons.

Manston's first RAF search and rescue unit was 'D' Flight of No. 22 Squadron which commenced operations in July 1961, flying Westland Whirlwind HAR.10 helicopters. These machines were fitted with Alvis Leonides Major piston-engines and were eight- to ten-seater general-purpose machines built to the basic design of the Sikorsky S–55 type.

During their stay at Manston, from 1950 to 1958, the USAF provided search and rescue facilities in the form of 'A' Flight of the 9th Air Rescue Squadron and the 66th Air Rescue Squadron at different periods. Both were equipped with these Grumman SA-16 Albatross amphibians and had access to the B-29 Superfortress adapted for long-range searches.

Opposite: Manston's Commanding Officer, Wg. Cdr. D.B. Wills DFC (left), presenting the citation of the Air Force Medal to Flt. Sgt. Ian Jones (from Birchington) in March 1968. The award resulted from gallant action by Jones in the previous September when a Whirlwind of No. 22 Squadron rendered aid to a German yawl in distress. Flt. Lts Laycock and Burningham look on.

A Sikorsky S–55 helicopter of the 66th Air Rescue Squadron being demonstrated to an admiring crowd in the 1950s, apparently at an open day at Manston. The USAF units were the first to operate helicopters in the search and rescue service in east Kent from their Manston base.

An impressive view of a Westland Wessex HC.2 at its Manston dispersal when serving with 'E' Flight of No. 22 Squadron in the late 1970s. XV730 was not built, originally, for search and rescue duties but was converted to that role. Note the squadron badge on the fin, incorporating the Greek letter 'P', symbol for Pi and adopted by the squadron in 1915.

An inspection of the FIDO (Fog Intensive Dispersal Operation) installation by a party of senior RAF officers in 1957. Fifteen UK airfields were fitted with this system of lifting fog above a runway by heat, generated when vapourized petrol was burned from a line of pipes running along both sides of the main runway.

Installations of the FIDO varied, with some having pipes above ground level, others having them recessed in channels, as at Manston. Becoming operational here in April 1945, it was the last FIDO in use and having safely landed more than 120 aircraft was closed down about 1959. Electronic landing aids had made the system obsolete.

The 'foam carpet' was introduced at Manston in 1964. This was a system which enabled aircraft with undercarriage damage or malfunction to land with wheels up without risk of fire as a foam carpet was pumped on to the runway smothering any sparks generated by the friction. This Canberra from Cottesmore successfully landed with the aid of foam on 30 April 1969.

A sheet of foam spray marks the passage of a Handley Page Victor 'V' bomber down the runway as it makes an emergency landing, caused by undercarriage trouble, at Manston, 8 January 1968. The large parachute has been deployed to provide braking during the aircraft's slide on its belly. Quite a number of Victor and other 'V' bombers were 'customers' of the foam landing system.

With a satisfactory conclusion (a controlled crash!) reached in this incident, the Victor sits on the runway surrounded by the usual airfield emergency vehicles while preparations are made for its removal. Worthy of note is how straight – despite the circumstances – the pilot has managed to keep the aircraft: not always achievable.

One of the four aircraft making use of the foam carpet in 1977 was this Blackburn Buccaneer. In its sixteen and a half years of operation the system assisted forty-four military and eighteen civilian machines to make safe landings. The types ranged in size from the Beagle Basset to various 'V' bombers and a DH Comet airliner.

An Avro 748 of Skyways, one of the many civil aircraft to make use of the foam carpet, lands without injury to the crew or twenty-six passengers on 9 May 1968. A maximum area of 3,600 × 90 ft, using 100,000 gallons of foam and costing £3,500, could be laid. A combination of technical and economic factors caused the system's withdrawal in October 1980.

Members of the Manston Fire Service undergoing routine practice in the 1970s. Those present are Messrs D. Duff, D. Sutter and A. Harris. The service was staffed by civilian firemen employed by the RAF. The uniform, it will be noted, differs considerably from that in use today.

A unique view of the crash/fire station in the 1970s. The photo is especially interesting as it shows all the services prepared for an actual emergency landing on the foam carpet. Both civilian (right) and RAF ambulances (left) are present with the fire-engines poised at the threshold of the building.

A bulk fuel tanker of the 1950s at Manston carrying, as the marking specifies, AVTAG (also known as JP–4), the aviation fuel with an additive. By this time high-pressure refuelling had superseded the Second World War bowsers and tanker capacities were in the 1,000 to 3,500 gallon range with a delivery rate of 500 gallons per minute.

The entrance and guard-room to the Second World War radar station at Sandwich. Relinquished by the RAF many years ago the site is now the scene of various commercial activities. The station was part of the UK radar chain for approximately fifteen years and played a major role in our air defence of south-east England from 1943 to 1945.

The Main Operations block as it appeared in 1993. This was a brick and concrete blockhouse opened in 1943. It swept to a range of 100 miles, between approximately 3,000 and 60,000 ft, and had an establishment of about 160 RAF and WAAF personnel. Various aerial arrays were located in the adjacent fields. In case of emergency a stand-by site existed at Sholden.

SECTION EIGHT

Miscellany

The 'Grand Flying Display' promoters of the 1920s and '30s were nomadic, numerous and very busy during the summer months of those years. This is a typical local press advertisement of the time and on this occasion the added attraction for potential Thanet customers was the presence of the two famous long-distance flyers, Amy Johnson and Jim Mollison.

Early flying days at what became Ramsgate Airport. The four-passenger DH.83 Fox Moth carries the colour scheme of Hillman Airways Ltd who commenced a Romford–Ramsgate service in June 1932. Three aircraft of this type superseded the similar number of Puss Moths which were originally employed.

The grave of Lt. Cdr. Eugene Esmonde VC, DSO in the Gillingham, Kent, cemetery. He was killed in heroic circumstances on 12 February 1942 when leading six Swordfish aircraft of No. 825 Squadron of the Fleet Air Arm, taking off from Manston. Their task was a torpedo attack on the German battle-cruisers *Scharnhorst* and *Gneisenau* and the cruiser *Prinz Eugen*.

For many years, apart from the First World War period, postcard views of areas and subjects of interest found a ready market both locally and with visitors. So far as security regulations permitted, RAF stations were quite often featured by commercial photographers. In this 1926 print the attractions of both village and camp are combined.

Occasional visitors to Manston were Bristol Britannias from No. 99 or No. 511 Squadrons of RAF Air Support Command. The aircraft shown is XM518. Entering service in 1959 the type could carry approximately 140 passengers and was fitted with four Bristol Proteus engines. Britannias were also widely used by civilian airlines.

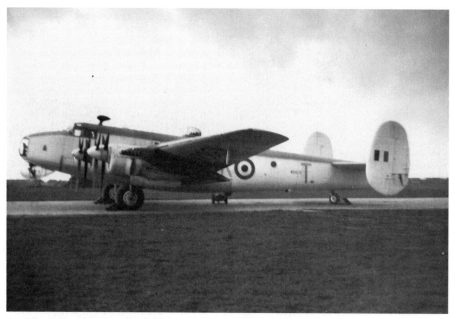

Another aircraft to make fleeting appearances at Manston was the long-range, maritime-reconnaissance Avro Shackleton, in service in this role from 1951 to 1962. In addition to patrols of long duration round UK shores from bases in Northern Ireland and south-west England, Shackletons operated out of Gibraltar and Malta. One of the type remained airborne for 24 hours and 21 minutes.

A Vickers Valiant high-speed, high-altitude bomber of the V-Force visits Manston on an air-day. The Valiant saw eventful service from 1955 to 1965, participating in the Suez campaign, dropping Britain's first atom and hydrogen bombs, forming part of NATO air forces and making a significant contribution to the development of refuelling in flight.

Air shows, displays or extravaganzas held at RAF Manston in past years have invariably included an exhibition by the Falcons, the RAF's own display parachutists. In recent years they have jumped from aircraft supplied by the RAF but on 12 October 1971 the Army's Red Devils descended from this civilian DH Rapide.

Personnel of the Minster ROC in 1942 (Royal Observer Corps since April 1941). Back row, left to right: F. Golder, J. Smith, E. Lewis, E. Spanton, P. Golder. Second row: J. White, R. Hammond, F. Winter, E. Chase, N. Smith. Front row: W. Petts, E. Butcher, P. Jezard, D. Bewden. Their A1 Post, in the background, was located on the A253 road abreast the main runway.

This Gloster Javelin, XH764, was on display from July 1967, for some years, at Manston. It was a high-performance, two-seater, all-weather fighter of the period from 1955 to 1967, during which it served with eighteen squadrons of the RAF in the UK and overseas. It was powered by two Armstrong Siddeley Sapphire engines and its production ran to 430 aircraft.

NO	SURNAME	NAMES	AGE	ADDRESS	TOWN	DESCRIPTION	ADMITTED 1940	DISCHARGED	TRANSFERRED 1940	
H 1054	OUSLEY	Gladys	16	15, Alexandra Road	Ramsgate	A	cas	24. Aug	24. Aug	PRESTON HALL	AIR RAID
H 1055	LUCAS	Alfred	69	82, Boundary Road	Ramsgate	A	cas	24. Aug	24. Aug	do	AIR RAID
H 1056	HILL	Alfred	27	1103933 A.C.2. S.H.Q.	R.A.F.	B	cas	24. Aug	24. Aug	do	
H 1057	STEAD	William	85	36, Park Road	Ramsgate	A	cas	24. Aug	25. Aug	do	AIR RAID
H 1058	THOMPSON	Charles	21	3601429/PTE. 'C' COY 6TH BN BORDER REGT		B	cas	24. Aug	24. Aug	do	
H 1059	BROOKER	James	23	2062695 GNR. 342 COY	R.E.	B	cas	24. Aug	25. Aug	UNIT	
H 1060	DEBENHAM	Kenneth	20	PILOT OFFICER 151, SQUADRON	R.A.F.	B	cas	24. Aug	26. Aug	HALTON	
H 1061	HUNTLEY	Donald	38	A.F.S. A.R.P.	Ramsgate	A	cas	24. Aug	25. Aug	HOME	AIR RAID
P. 1402	COOK	Frederick	45	103, Winstanley bros.	Ramsgate	A	cas	25. Aug		HOME	AIR RAID
P. 1403	DEBLING	William	43	13, Montefiore Cottages	Ramsgate	A	cas	25. Aug		HOME	AIR RAID
P. 1404	MEDHURST	Mabel	18	17, Station Approach Rd	Ramsgate	A	cas	25. Aug		HOME	AIR RAID
H.T. 148 P. 1405	ALLEN	Ernest	56	50, Chilton Lane	Ramsgate	A	cas	25. Aug		HOME	AIR RAID
P. 1406	PHILPOT	Rose	47	65, Winstanley bros.	Ramsgate	A	cas	25. Aug		HOME	AIR RAID
P. 1408	JOHNSTONE	A	43	3902162 PTE 521 COAST BATTERY		B	cas	25. Aug		UNIT	
Ray 1085	RAWLINGS	James	40	D33415 PTE H.D. 6TH BN. BUFFS		B	sick	25. Aug		UNIT PRESTON	
H 1064	SAYER	William	72	26, Woodford Ave.	Ramsgate	A	cas	26. Aug	27. Aug	HALL	AIR RAID
H 1065	EFFMERT	Willi	24	29/51596 FELDWEBEL GERMAN AIR FORCE		B	cas	26. Aug	30. Aug	ROYAL HERBERT HOSPITAL WOOLWICH	ESSMERT GERMAN 7/46
H 1066	WALKER	William	27	PILOT OFFICER 616, SQUADRON	R.A.F.	B	cas	26. Aug	27. Aug	R.A.F. HOSPITAL HALTON	
P. 412	GOLDFINCH	Thomas	60	8, Victoria Road	Ramsgate	A	cas	26. Aug		HOME S.I.Q.	AIR RAID
P. 416	YOUNG	Ronald	19	909550 A.C.1. FLIGHT, S.H.Q. 12 SERVICING	R.A.F.	B	cas	27. Aug	27. Aug	MANSTON	
P. 418	SKINNER	Alfred	23	4619905 PTE. ANTI-TANK COY 198TH INFANTRY BRIGADE 8TH (IRISH)		B	sick	27. Aug		UNIT	
P. 1421	DOBSON	Joseph	23	PTE. 9TH KINGS H.M.D. DUCLIDGDLB		B	sick	27. Aug		UNIT R.N.	
Ray 1090	GARNER	Victor	21	SEAMAN R.M. PATROL 90- FERVENT		B	cas	27. Aug		SICK BAY	
Ray 1091	COOK	Raymond	21	28, Station App. Road	Ramsgate	A	cas	27. Aug		HOME	AIR RAID
H.T. 142	LURCOOK	George	19	110, Herson Road	Ramsgate	A	cas	27. Aug		HOME	AIR RAID
H.T. 143	CHANDLER	William	48	43, Napleton Road	Ramsgate	A	cas	27. Aug		HOME	

An extract from the Ramsgate Hospital register covering the period from 24 to 27 August 1940. Except for three, all were 'casualties' as opposed to 'sick' cases and included Army, Navy, RAF (pilots and ground crew) and civilian personnel together with one German airman. Note the predominance of cases due to the air raids at that time. The name of the German (from the crew of a destroyed Dornier bomber) was Essmert and not Effmert as incorrectly recorded.

Two former adversaries meet at Manston. In the cockpit of Manston's Spitfire, TB752, sits Adolf Galland, former commander of II/JG26 during the Battle of Britain. In 1940 Reichsmarschall Göring asked Galland what help he could give him to defeat the RAF. Galland's famous reply was, 'a Staffel of Spitfires Herr Reichsmarschall'. Galland visited Manston in 1983 and had to make do with a single Spitfire, not a 'Staffel'.